D1206786

THE VACCINATION
DEBATE

BY REBECCA RISSMAN

CONTENT CONSULTANT
Jonah B. Sacha, PhD
Vaccine & Gene Therapy Institute
Oregon Health & Science University

Essential Library

An Imprint of Abdo Publishing | abdopublishing.com

abdopublishing.com

Published by Abdo Publishing, a division of ABDO, PO Box 398166, Minneapolis, Minnesota 55439. Copyright © 2016 by Abdo Consulting Group, Inc. International copyrights reserved in all countries. No part of this book may be reproduced in any form without written permission from the publisher. Essential Library™ is a trademark and logo of Abdo Publishing.

Printed in the United States of America, North Mankato, Minnesota
082015
012016

THIS BOOK CONTAINS
RECYCLED MATERIALS

Cover Photo: Philip Nealey/Somos Images/Corbis
Interior Photos: Frederic J. Brown/AFP/Getty Images, 5; AP Images, 9; Sang Tan/ AP Images, 11; Rich Pedroncelli/AP Images, 15, 89; Three Lions/Getty Images, 17; Corbis, 19; Media for Medical/UIG/Getty Images, 23; David Massey/Daytona Beach News-Journal/AP Images, 29; ImagineChina/AP Images, 32; David Cheskin/PA Wire/ AP Images, 37; Jose Luis Magana/AP Images, 44; Shehzad Noorani/Canadian Press/ AP Images, 47; Nicholas Kamm/AFP/Getty Images, 51; Xinhua/AP Images, 54; Chen Xichun/ImagineChina/AP Images, 59; Alex Duval Smith/Picture-Alliance/DPA/AP Images, 61; Keith Srakocic/AP Images, 62; Mandel Ngan/AFP/Getty Images, 65; Centers for Disease Control and Prevention, 67; Brendan Smialowski/AFP/Getty Images, 69; John Locher/AP Images, 73; Damian Dovarganes/AP Images, 77; Thony Belizaire/AFP/Getty Images, 79; Bilgin S. Sasmaz/Anadolu Agency/Getty Images, 84; Bernd von Jutrczenka/DPA/Corbis, 87; Steve Yeater/AP Images, 91; Hank Morgan/ Rainbow/Science Faction/Corbis, 95; John Moore/Getty Images, 97; Tony Talbot/AP Images, 99

Editor: Arnold Ringstad
Series Designer: Maggie Villaume

Library of Congress Control Number: 2015944924

Cataloging-in-Publication Data

Rissman, Rebecca.
 The vaccination debate / Rebecca Rissman.
  p. cm. -- (Special reports)
 ISBN 978-1-62403-905-8 (lib. bdg.)
 Includes bibliographical references and index.
 1. Vaccination--Juvenile literature. 2. Vaccination--Public opinion--Juvenile literature. I. Title.
 614.4/7--dc23

                                                                          2015944924

CONTENTS

CHAPTER ONE

THE
OUTBREAK

In the year 2000, measles was declared eliminated from the United States. This meant the highly contagious disease, which causes rashes and a high fever, no longer spread within the country. Vaccines had resulted in measles's decline. However, other nations still suffered from outbreaks. In the 2010s, approximately 20 million people around the world contracted measles each year.[1] This meant international travel could still bring measles to the United States. However, due to the country's high vaccination rate, doctors did not worry about the disease spreading. By 2001, only approximately 100 to 200 US cases of measles were reported each year.[2] Health officials

Health officials urged the public to get vaccinated against measles in early 2015.

Measles is highly contagious.

THE BEST WAY TO
PROTECT YOURSELF
IS TO GET VACCINATED.

Ask your health care provider today
if you need a measles vaccine.

For more information visit
publichealth.lacounty.gov
www.publichealth.lacounty.gov

Public Health

considered this number low and manageable. However, in 2014, the number of measles cases spiked to 668.[3] Experts wondered if an outbreak was on the horizon. Then, it happened.

Between December 2014 and January 2015, doctors in southern California saw a sudden influx of patients suffering from measles. In the following weeks, people throughout the country were diagnosed with the disease. The Centers for Disease Control and Prevention (CDC), a US government organization that tracks and contains diseases, quickly traced the outbreak back to its origins. It appeared to have begun at the popular theme park Disneyland, located in Anaheim, California. An infected park visitor had spread the sickness to other visitors and park employees. These

JUST HOW CONTAGIOUS IS MEASLES?

Measles is often called the most contagious virus on Earth. There are many reasons for this, but one of the biggest has to do with where the virus can live. Measles is a respiratory disease. Respiratory diseases are spread through coughing and sneezing. Many respiratory viruses live deep in the lungs. But measles is found in the nose and at the very top of the trachea, or windpipe. This means if a person coughs or sneezes, the measles virus easily exits the body.

The measles virus can also live outside of a human for two hours. This means an infected person who has touched a surface or simply breathed into a room has made those areas contagious for two hours. Measles is so contagious experts estimate 90 percent of nonimmune people who are exposed to the virus will become ill.[4]

people then spread it on to others. By mid-February, 141 people in 17 states and Washington, DC, had been diagnosed with the potentially fatal disease.[5]

Many people wondered how this could have happened in the age of vaccination. Vaccines enable peoples' immune systems to resist illnesses. They are often administered by needle injections, pills, or nasal sprays. They are available for many different diseases, and the measles vaccine is still in widespread use. Doctors give babies and young children many vaccines to protect them from harmful diseases they may encounter later in life. People who have received vaccinations for a disease are said to be immunized against that disease. Over the past century, vaccines against deadly diseases have saved millions of lives.

DEVELOPING THE MMR VACCINE

The measles vaccine was first used in the United States in 1963. Before that, the country had more than 400,000 cases of measles each year.[6] The illness caused symptoms that ranged from a runny nose, rash, and high fever to serious ear problems that occasionally resulted

DOUBTING THE DANGER FROM MEASLES

Not everyone responded to the measles outbreak with fear. Many vaccine skeptics pointed to the fact that while measles causes hundreds of thousands of deaths in other countries, no Americans have died from measles in the last decade. And while measles can be a very serious disease, it is usually not life threatening for people living in countries with advanced medical care. Vaccine skeptics emphasized that most Americans suffering from measles experience a fever, flu-like symptoms, and a rash. While unpleasant, these symptoms are not often deadly.

Health officials disagreed. They noted that as many as one-third of people with measles need to be hospitalized, and they explained when complications of the disease arise, they are often very serious.

in deafness. In extreme cases, measles caused lung infections, brain swelling, and even death. In the decades after US children began receiving the measles vaccine, measles rates dropped by 99 percent.[7] It seemed to many as though measles was no longer a threat.

In 1971, the measles vaccine was combined with vaccines for two other diseases: mumps and rubella. The resulting measles, mumps, rubella (MMR) vaccine was highly successful. One dose of the MMR vaccine, given to one-year-olds, was 93 percent effective against measles. After the second dose, given between the ages of four and six, the vaccine was 97 percent effective.[8] Physicians felt confident measles, mumps, and rubella were no longer global threats.

The development of a measles vaccine in 1963 led to the disease's elimination in the United States by the turn of the century.

FROM THE HEADLINES

AUTISM AND THE MMR VACCINE

In 1998, British physician Andrew Wakefield published controversial research in the scientific medical journal the *Lancet*. The paper claimed the MMR vaccine had very harmful side effects. It suggested the vaccine could cause intestinal problems. It further claimed those intestinal problems could lead to brain disorders, including autism.

Autism affects approximately 1 in every 68 US children.[9] The disorder, which can vary widely in severity, impairs social interaction and communication skills. Symptoms of autism often begin to appear at the age of 15 to 18 months. The MMR vaccine is typically given to infants at 12 to 15 months. The close proximity of the vaccine and appearance of autism symptoms made many wonder if the disorder could be linked to the vaccine. Wakefield's paper added to this fear. In response, vaccination rates in the United States and the United Kingdom dropped.

Many Hollywood celebrities made Wakefield's work famous. Television personality Jenny McCarthy talked at length about how her son's autism appeared

Even after scientists disputed Wakefield's findings, he continued to find support in the anti-vaccine community.

shortly after his MMR vaccination. She believed the vaccine was responsible for his condition.

However, experts soon disproved Wakefield's findings. Many other studies showed a link between the MMR vaccine and autism does not exist. A close review of Wakefield's work revealed he had altered some of his data to fit his predetermined conclusion. He had also received money from a company developing a competing vaccine. Before long, Wakefield was stripped of his medical license and the *Lancet* retracted his paper. However, the impact of his work had already affected people around the world.

In just a few years, Wakefield went from being a respected doctor to being a target for blame. The reduced vaccination rate spurred by his paper resulted in the reemergence of many previously controlled diseases, such as whooping cough and measles.

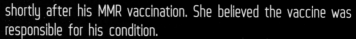

"IT IS REALLY A BAD COMBINATION WHEN YOU HAVE PEOPLE THAT TRIVIALIZE WHAT CAN BE A VERY DANGEROUS ILLNESS AND THEN, ON BAD INFORMATION, DECIDE THAT VACCINES ARE UNSAFE."[11]

—DR. GIL CHAVEZ, STATE EPIDEMIOLOGIST FOR CALIFORNIA

OPTING OUT OF VACCINES

The dramatic reduction in measles cases enabled by vaccines made the Disneyland outbreak especially shocking. The resurgence of the disease highlighted the fact that not all Americans vaccinate their children. In fact, approximately 5 percent of kindergarteners in the United States have not received the measles vaccination.[10] This is not because vaccines are expensive or difficult to get. Health insurance or government assistance programs pay for nearly all vaccinations in the United States. Families who cannot afford vaccines can often get them for free. Access to vaccines is easy throughout the country.

Instead, many Americans actively choose not to vaccinate. They do this for a variety of reasons. Some people have religious motives for avoiding vaccinations. Some members of the Dutch Reformed Church, for example, believe vaccinations may affect the way a believer interacts with God. They recommend their church members do not get vaccinations or vaccinate their children.

Other people cannot be vaccinated for medical reasons. People whose immune systems have been weakened by diseases such as HIV or cancer are often not able to get vaccines. This is because the vaccines require a fully functioning immune system. Doctors also recommend that very young infants and pregnant women avoid certain vaccinations.

Most people who do not vaccinate make their decision because they believe vaccines may be unsafe. They fear some ingredients in vaccines are unnecessary or could be harmful. Others worry about the side effects of vaccines. Some feel vaccines cause other serious diseases that can

VACCINATION STATIONS

In many developed countries, such as the United States and the United Kingdom, vaccines are available in multiple locations to make them easy to access. Patients can get a vaccine while visiting their doctor at a hospital or clinic. They can also get a vaccine at a drugstore or pharmacy. Some areas even have mobile vaccination stations, mini-clinics set up specifically to administer vaccines. These are often found temporarily in churches, schools, or other community centers.

Some rural communities have gotten creative about distributing vaccines. In Marion County, West Virginia, health-care professionals drive a mobile home stocked with vaccines around the countryside. Marion County residents responded positively to the vaccination mobile home. Health officials vaccinated more than 200 people in just ten hours during their first trip through the county.[12]

otherwise be avoided. Despite a lack of evidence for these claims, the group of people with these beliefs is growing in the United States. Many experts believe unvaccinated people were responsible for the Disneyland measles outbreak. If people continue opting out of vaccines, public health officials worry other now-rare diseases could make a resurgence.

"THERE IS EVERY REASON TO GET VACCINATED—THERE AREN'T REASONS TO NOT."[13]

—PRESIDENT BARACK OBAMA

Some people believe vaccines cause autism, and they feel this is a bigger danger than the diseases vaccines protect against, such as measles.

CHAPTER TWO

A HISTORY OF
CONTROVERSY

Controversies have surrounded vaccines for as long as they have existed. Debates have raged about their safety, validity, and necessity. When British doctor Edward Jenner created the first successful vaccine in 1796, his work was not universally celebrated. Rather, it was met with skepticism.

Jenner knew dairymaids who worked with cows often contracted a disease called cowpox. The dairymaids who had recovered from cowpox tended not to get smallpox, a deadly disease affecting humans. Jenner discovered he could take the fluid from a human patient's cowpox sore and inject it into another person as a way to protect against smallpox. The cowpox fluid triggered the person's immune system to build

Jenner's development of vaccines saved many lives, but it quickly attracted controversy.

up defenses against both cowpox and smallpox. Jenner's vaccine worked, yet the idea behind it terrified some people. The fact that the pus from a cowpox blister could keep people from becoming ill was confusing or revolting to many.

Some of the biggest objections to Jenner's vaccine came from concerned parents and religious leaders. Parents worried about the potential side effects of transferring pus from a sick person to their healthy children. Clergy preached that vaccines were religiously improper because they involved transferring fluid that originated in animal tissue into humans. Cowpox was a disease that was transmitted from cows to people. Therefore, the clergy argued, it contained animal matter. In the late 1800s, several anti-vaccination groups were established. They published pamphlets warning people vaccinations were unnecessary and dangerous. They also claimed being forced to vaccinate infringed on a person's freedom.

Scientists developed new vaccines and gained a deeper understanding of how they work. By introducing a weakened virus to a person's body, the immune system learns how to combat that virus. Later, if the body encounters the full-strength virus, the immune system already has defenses in place to ward it off.

In the 1900s, more people became accepting of vaccines. This shift in popular opinion was highlighted during World War II (1939–1945). By this time, scientists had developed vaccines for several infectious diseases, including smallpox, diphtheria, tetanus, pertussis, and influenza. Military leaders fighting on both sides of the

Soldiers across the globe received vaccines during World War II.

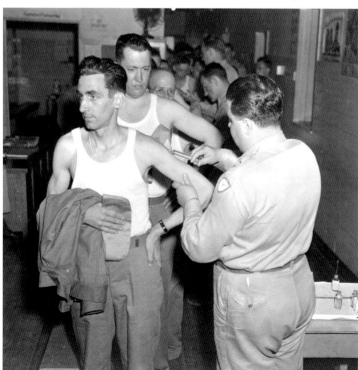

conflict wanted to prevent unnecessary casualties from common diseases, so they launched vaccination programs for soldiers. Troops from Germany, the United Kingdom, France, and the United States were all given vaccines to keep them as healthy as possible while they fought.

In the United States, vaccination suddenly became a sign of patriotism. Getting a vaccine became associated with supporting the war effort. More and more Americans chose to vaccinate their children and become vaccinated themselves.

THE PRESIDENT'S POLIO

In 1921, polio, the most feared epidemic of the early 1900s, struck rising political star Franklin D. Roosevelt. At that time, there was no vaccine for the disease. Roosevelt and his family worried about what it could mean for his future. People with polio can suffer from complications that cause weakness in the muscles, paralysis, and even death.

Roosevelt was soon paralyzed in both legs. Still, he continued his political career, becoming governor of New York in 1929 and president of the United States in 1933. He became the only president to use a wheelchair extensively. Roosevelt worked with charity groups to fund polio vaccine research.

THE GOVERNMENT GETS INVOLVED

Polio is a serious, contagious disease. It can cause paralysis, breathing difficulties, and even death. Thousands of cases were reported each year in the United States throughout the early 1900s. Researchers hunted for a vaccine to put a stop to polio. Doctors Jonas Salk and Albert Sabin finally developed vaccines for it in the 1950s. The demand was so great the US government had to ration the vaccines to make sure supplies could last. By the late 1960s, researchers had developed vaccines for measles, mumps, and rubella.

In the following years, scientists continued creating new vaccines. They also improved existing ones. Many parents were thrilled. They felt they were protecting their children from diseases that had hurt, disabled, and even killed so many people from their own generation. The US government encouraged this acceptance of vaccines. It began focusing on preventative health care. This meant that instead of using its resources to treat illnesses, the government would use resources to stop people from becoming ill in the first place.

Medical professionals knew many children passed germs and diseases along at school. Many states had already passed laws requiring children to be vaccinated in order to attend school. Some of these laws had come as early as the late 1800s. However, few of these laws were being enforced. Unvaccinated children were still bringing illnesses into schools and causing outbreaks. In the 1960s and 1970s, states began enforcing these laws in response to measles outbreaks that threatened public health.

By the late 1960s and early 1970s, vaccinations had reduced the rate of common and deadly diseases drastically in the United States. Measles rates, for example, had dropped by half in states with required school vaccinations.[1] The smallpox vaccine had been so successful it was no longer recommended by physicians because it was considered unnecessary. The smallpox vaccine had effectively eliminated the disease. Some scientists were so optimistic about the future of vaccines they predicted a world entirely free of infectious disease. However, doubts about vaccines soon crept back into the public consciousness.

DTP AND SERIOUS COMPLICATIONS

In the 1970s, an international controversy erupted around the vaccine DTP. This vaccination immunized children against three diseases: diphtheria, tetanus, and pertussis, commonly known as whooping cough. The combined vaccine had been in use since 1948. A report out of a

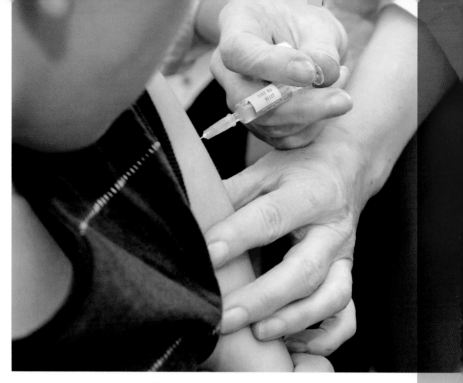

The DTP vaccine is given as a shot in the arm.

hospital in London, England, claimed 36 children had

suffered neurological problems as a result of receiving

the vaccine.[2] Before long, the story was being told in

newspapers and on television. Anti-vaccine groups,

such as the Association of Parents of Vaccine-Damaged

Children, gained international attention. Fear swept across

the globe.

Following the British report about the DTP shot,

vaccine rates in the United Kingdom dropped. Many

people were skeptical about the safety of the vaccine. Even

British physicians were unsure whether the vaccine was

safe. Prominent doctor Gordon Stewart published his own

findings linking neurological problems in children to the DTP vaccine. This contributed to the spreading distrust of vaccines.

As more and more people avoided the DTP vaccine, the diseases it prevented began spreading again. Three major outbreaks of pertussis swept through the United Kingdom. British medical professionals scrambled to reassure parents the vaccine was safe. Several studies disproved the theory that the DTP vaccine caused neurological problems.

Fears about the DTP vaccine also spread in the United States. Several lawsuits were filed against DTP vaccine manufacturers. While there was a lack of evidence supporting the claims that the vaccine caused injuries, the people who sued vaccine manufacturers were

VACCINE ROULETTE

Fears about the DTP vaccine—also known as the DPT vaccine—spread to the United States in the 1980s. In 1982, a documentary called *DPT: Vaccine Roulette* was released by a television station in Washington, DC. It focused on the side effects, including brain damage, which appeared to occur in a very small percentage of children who received the vaccine. Its message was very frightening. It told parents to be wary of vaccines and the side effects they could cause.

However, the information found in *Vaccine Roulette* was very one-sided. Many critics noted the documentary paid little attention to the seriousness of one of the diseases the vaccine prevented: pertussis.

This documentary highlighted the debate surrounding the DTP vaccine and made many people nervous about vaccines in general. Soon after its release, a new wave of anti-vaccination sentiment emerged in public debates.

awarded financial damages. This made many people feel the vaccine manufacturers were admitting guilt.

In response to the confusion and controversy surrounding the DTP vaccine, the US Congress passed the National Childhood Vaccine Injury Act (NCVIA) in 1986. This act ensured major health-oriented agencies, such as the CDC and the National Institutes of Health, coordinated all vaccine-related activities. It required medical professionals who administer vaccines to educate their patients about vaccines first. Doctors were asked to record any vaccine side effects their patients experienced. The goal of the NCVIA was to reassure and educate people about vaccines.

FEARS ABOUT VACCINES

In the 1980s, a new vaccine for the disease hepatitis B joined the growing list of recommended immunizations. As the list of vaccinations grew, some people worried about the consequences of administering so many different vaccines. By that time, vaccines protected children from diphtheria, measles, mumps, rubella, tetanus, pertussis, polio, and a bacterium called Haemophilus influenzae type B (HIB). The HIB vaccine prevented serious infections such as pneumonia. Though some of these vaccines were delivered in combination shots, the number of injections children needed to be fully immunized was still high. Some vaccines even required multiple shots in order to be effective. Concerned parents wondered if the volume of vaccines was safe and if they had all been thoroughly tested.

In 1998, British physician Andrew Wakefield published an inflammatory study. It suggested a link between the MMR vaccine and autism spectrum disorder. This paper caused the biggest wave of anti-vaccine outrage in history. While the scientific community quickly dismissed Wakefield's claims, his work created a lasting impression on many. More and more parents felt fearful of vaccines. A growing number of people chose to

VACCINE SCHEDULES

Each year, health industry leaders endorse a list of recommended vaccines for all children. This list is called a vaccine schedule. Each vaccine comes with its own individual timeline. Some are given once, at a certain age. Others are given in multiple doses over the course of a year or more. For example, the DTP vaccine is usually given in five doses: at two months, four months, six months, fifteen to eighteen months, and again at four to six years.

In the 1940s, the vaccine schedule was relatively short. It included vaccines for smallpox, tetanus, diphtheria, and pertussis. By 2010, the schedule had grown significantly, protecting children from 14 different diseases. Children following this vaccine schedule may get up to 23 shots in their first year of life.[3]

ask for vaccine exemptions when enrolling their children in schools that required vaccines. These exemptions allow parents to cite religious, medical, or philosophical reasons to not vaccinate their children.

Today, the vast majority of children in the United States get the recommended vaccinations. However, pockets of unvaccinated children exist in areas all over the country. Even though the evidence shows vaccines are safe, political debates continue to rage around the subject of vaccination.

"I SHOULD THINK THERE WOULD BE MORE CHANCE OF YOUR CHILD CHOKING TO DEATH ON A CHOCOLATE BAR THAN OF BECOMING SERIOUSLY ILL FROM A MEASLES IMMUNIZATION. SO WHAT ON EARTH ARE YOU WORRYING ABOUT? IT REALLY IS ALMOST A CRIME TO ALLOW YOUR CHILD TO GO UNIMMUNIZED."[4]

—AUTHOR ROALD DAHL, WRITING IN 1986 ABOUT HIS DAUGHTER'S DEATH FROM MEASLES IN 1962

CHAPTER THREE

VACCINE ISSUES AND HERD IMMUNITY

Immunity is the body's ability to recognize and fight off an infection. The immune system works hard to keep the body healthy. People who are immune to a disease have developed proteins called antibodies to fight that disease. The body only produces antibodies after it has been exposed to a disease. The antibodies a body produces for one disease are unique. They cannot be used to fight another disease.

There are two different types of immunity. A person develops active immunity through vaccination or by becoming ill with the actual disease. Babies develop

Getting vaccinated provides a person with the antibodies needed to fight off a particular disease.

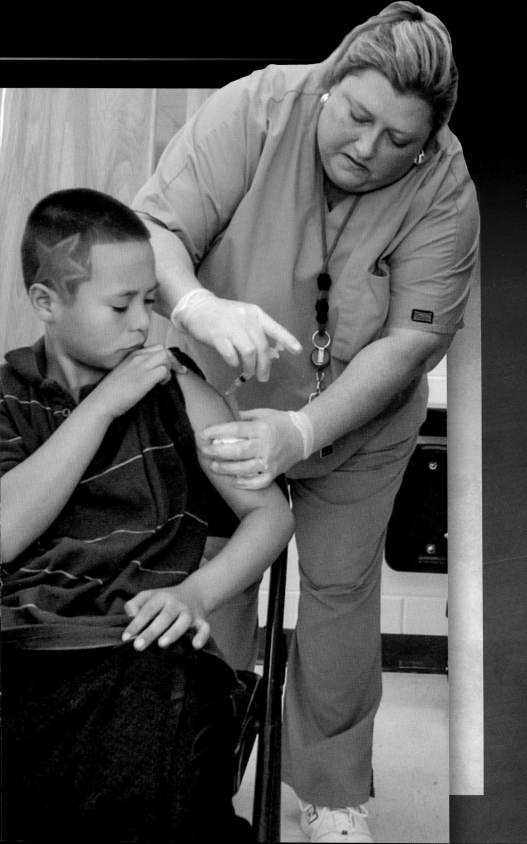

A DOCTOR'S ROLE

Many parents rely on a physician to advise them on what is best for their children. Doctors help parents decide when to potty train, when to introduce new foods, and even how to get a child to sleep through the night.

It is not surprising, then, that many doctors heavily influence parents' decision about vaccines. Parents who take their children to doctors who are pro-vaccine are more likely to vaccinate their children. Parents who take their children to doctors who are skeptical about vaccines, or who advise parents to administer vaccines on a delayed schedule, are more likely to follow this advice.

passive immunity when they get antibodies that are passed from their mothers. This type of immunity typically only lasts for six to eight months after birth.

ISSUES WITH VACCINES

While vaccines are an effective way to make people immune to diseases, they are not perfect. One issue is that many people cannot be vaccinated for medical reasons. Pregnant women and very young children cannot receive some types of vaccinations. This is because receiving the vaccine might overwhelm their immune systems or make them unwell. Very sick people, those undergoing organ transplants, and those receiving certain cancer treatments also cannot be safely vaccinated. This is because they could become ill from a vaccine that contains a weakened live virus, or because their immune systems might not respond to the vaccine as they should.

Both vaccines and exposure to diseases provide active immunity. However, the immunity a person develops from being exposed to an actual disease is often more effective than what they develop when they are vaccinated. People who are vaccinated against a disease often need to receive multiple doses of the vaccine in order to be protected for their entire lives, while they may only need to be exposed to the real disease once in order to develop lifelong immunity.

Another problem with vaccines is that in very rare instances, vaccines themselves can make people ill. While it is impossible for vaccines made with dead viruses to infect a person with that disease, vaccines made from weakened viruses could potentially cause an illness. However, scientists stress that when this happens, the

SICK FROM THE POLIO VACCINE

In 1955, 200 children became ill with polio after receiving the polio vaccine. Ten died from the disease.[1] An investigation showed the vaccine they were given contained the live polio virus. Normally this would be fine, because the drug company that produced the vaccine would have made the live virus inactive. However, something had gone wrong during the production of the vaccine, and the drug company's attempts to inactivate the virus had failed. When news of this incident spread, many people became nervous about giving their children vaccines. They grew distrustful of the drug companies behind vaccines.

Some flu vaccine production techniques use enormous numbers of eggs.

disease is much weaker than it would be if it were passed from an infected person.

Some people cannot get vaccines because they are allergic to some of their ingredients. Vaccines often contain additives that help them work more effectively. Some additives include allergens, such as egg material. The flu vaccine often includes eggs. Egg allergies are extremely common in young children. Those with severe egg allergies cannot receive the usual flu shot, though some new vaccines have been developed that do not use eggs in their production.

MORE TO THE
STORY

DOES THE FLU VACCINE GIVE YOU THE FLU?

Many people complain about flu-like symptoms shortly after getting the flu vaccine. A common explanation for this is that the vaccine contains the flu virus, which means it can actually give people the flu. This is incorrect.

Flu vaccines can be administered with a needle injection or a nasal spray. Neither type can cause the flu. Injected flu vaccines are made with dead flu virus or no flu virus at all. Nasal vaccines are made with weakened flu virus that is not strong enough to cause a flu infection.

When people experience mild reactions to a vaccine, such as fatigue, body aches, or fever, it is usually simply because their immune systems are reacting to a foreign substance. Studies have shown people given shots of the flu vaccine and people given shots of salt water have reported nearly all the same symptoms. The only difference in side effects experienced by the two groups was that the group who got the flu vaccine reported more soreness and redness at their injection site.

Sometimes people do become ill after receiving their flu vaccine. The most common explanation for this is they contracted a different type of illness that caused flu-like symptoms around the same time they received their vaccine. Another explanation is they were exposed to the flu virus before they were vaccinated. Yet another explanation is they were infected by a strain of the flu the vaccine does not protect against.

TRAVEL AND VACCINES

In some areas of the world, diseases are rare among local people even though there is no herd immunity. Instead, the majority of the population has encountered the disease through infection and has developed active immunity to it. For people traveling into these areas, special vaccinations are often recommended.

For example, people traveling to some areas of South America and Africa are often urged to get the yellow fever vaccine. Travelers going to south Asia are often encouraged to get a vaccination for typhoid fever.

Finally, vaccines can cause side effects. Most side effects are mild, such as soreness at the injection site or fatigue. In rare cases, though, they can be serious. Rare vaccine side effects can include fever, nausea, headaches, and even seizures.

HERD IMMUNITY

Herd immunity is the concept that if a large proportion of a population has been vaccinated against a certain disease, that disease will spread more slowly and less widely than it would if fewer people were vaccinated. Many contagious diseases are passed from person to person. Herd immunity works because the chain of infection, or the passage of a disease from one person to another to another, is more likely to break if the majority of a population is vaccinated against that disease. Vaccinated people block off potential paths through which the disease can spread.

For some diseases, the percentage of vaccinated people needs to be quite high for herd immunity to be effective. Highly contagious diseases, such as measles, require approximately 92 to 94 percent of the population to be vaccinated.[2] Other diseases require much lower numbers. The seasonal flu only needs approximately 60 percent of a population to be vaccinated for herd immunity to function.[3]

As the number of people choosing not to vaccinate grows, however, scientists say herd immunity is threatened. They warn contagious diseases could cause a harmful outbreak if too many people are not vaccinated. In some areas, such as Los Angeles, California, the percentage of kindergarteners who are vaccinated against measles is near the herd immunity threshold for that disease. This places the population at risk for an outbreak.

"WHEN YOU HAVE ONLY AN EXTREMELY SMALL PROPORTION OF THE POPULATION VULNERABLE [TO A DISEASE], HERD IMMUNITY WILL PROTECT THEM. . . . WHEN YOU HAVE A SUBSTANTIAL PROPORTION, LIKE THE 10%-PLUS THAT WE'RE SEEING IN CERTAIN COMMUNITIES IN CALIFORNIA, THEN HERD IMMUNITY DOESN'T WORK VERY WELL."[4]

—ANTHONY FAUCI, DIRECTOR OF THE NATIONAL INSTITUTE OF ALLERGY AND INFECTIOUS DISEASE, DISCUSSING THE DISNEY MEASLES OUTBREAK OF 2014

CHAPTER FOUR

VACCINES AND
POPULAR
CULTURE

I n 2009, a group of health-care workers gathered outside the New York State capitol building in Albany with signs and posters. They were protesting the state government's requirement that they be vaccinated against influenza virus H1N1, which causes the disease commonly called the swine flu. The vaccine was relatively new, and it had been created quickly in comparison to other vaccines. Many of these health-care workers felt unsure about the potential side effects. Others felt upset they were being forced to get the vaccine without being given a choice about it. One

The 2009 swine flu vaccination effort prompted a wide range of responses for a variety of reasons.

nurse wondered aloud, "If something happens to me, if I get seriously injured from this vaccine, who's going to help me?"[1]

The number of people around the globe who are skeptical about vaccines has grown in the early 2000s. The majority of these people list three major reasons for their hesitancy. First, they worry vaccines are unsafe. Second, they believe vaccines are unnecessary. And third, they believe being forced to vaccinate is a violation of their freedom. These people's beliefs lead them to take a variety of actions. Some simply choose to learn more about how each vaccine works. They may do research online or ask their physician for advice. Other people accept some vaccines and reject others.

A small percentage of people who oppose vaccines

THE INTERNET AND VACCINES

Some people point to the Internet as one of the biggest contributors to the increasing prominence of the anti-vaccine movement. They claim people are swayed by the articles and comments they read online. Some medical professionals worry the information these people encounter online may not be reliable. Members of the anti-vaccine movement set up their own websites to actively share their beliefs.

At the same time, some pro-vaccine advocates feel the Internet is a great resource for those who would not otherwise have access to information about vaccines. People who are curious about vaccines can find reputable websites where they can learn about modern vaccines and their importance.

have stronger beliefs about the practice of vaccination itself. They often believe no vaccinations are safe and they should all be avoided. Some believe the health-care organizations that create vaccination recommendations have misled the public about vaccine safety and necessity. Though anti-vaccination proponents are a relatively small group of people, they often gain attention from the media.

REPORTING VACCINE INJURIES

Anti-vaccination advocates are not the only people interested in the safety of vaccines. Scientists also point to the importance of monitoring the effects of vaccines. Two major health organizations, the CDC and the Food and Drug Administration (FDA), created the Vaccine Adverse Event Reporting System (VAERS) in 1990. This organization exists to track any negative effects of vaccines.

Though it was created by health organizations heavily involved with vaccine production and regulation, VAERS strives to be a neutral party in the vaccine debate. Anyone can report an incident to VAERS, including parents, teachers, or health-care workers. However, just because VAERS catalogs an incident, this does not mean the incident was definitely the result of a vaccine. The CDC follows up on the reports to find out whether vaccines caused the incident.

Annually, VAERS receives approximately 30,000 reports of negative reactions to vaccines.[2] Some people interpret this number differently than others. Anti-vaccine advocates believe the figure proves they have valid concerns about vaccine safety. Pro-vaccine advocates note that 30,000 is a tiny fraction of the millions of vaccinations carried out each year. Additionally, they point out that the reporting and investigation of these incidents shows scientists take vaccine safety seriously.

WHERE VACCINE QUESTIONERS LIVE

In the last few decades, anti-vaccine sentiment has centered in the United States and Europe. Those who delay or avoid vaccinations for themselves and their children are often educated, middle- or upper-middle-class people. Some scientists note that these communities of people have never seen outbreaks of contagious disease firsthand, leaving them unaware of the serious consequences of these diseases. Others argue these populations have done their research and are entitled to make their own decisions about their health care.

However, not all resistance to vaccines is found in wealthy, developed nations. The pockets of vaccine skeptics found in other regions of the globe offer a revealing look into the variety of reasons people choose to opt out of vaccines. In Nigeria, for example, a 2003 boycott of government-sponsored vaccines occurred. The Nigerians who protested these vaccines did not do so because they were worried about the side effects of the vaccines or because they wanted a different vaccine schedule. Rather, they boycotted the vaccines and other government initiatives as a way to protest poor government treatment.

CLUSTERS AND CELEBRITIES

Around the globe, people who choose to opt out of or delay vaccines are often found in clusters. These are groups who share doubts about

"IT WOULD BE BETTER IF SCATTERED INDIVIDUALS WERE THE QUESTIONERS, BECAUSE WHEN THEY START CLUSTERING, IT BECOMES A BIGGER PROBLEM."[3]

—HEIDI LARSON, RESEARCHER AT THE LONDON SCHOOL OF HYGIENE AND TROPICAL MEDICINE

RELIGIOUS CLUSTERS

Some clusters of people who do not vaccinate have religious reasons to avoid immunizations. Some religions believe it is problematic to use human tissue in vaccines. They do not believe such tissue should be injected into people. Some religions object to other substances used in vaccines, such as animal tissue.

In order to make some vaccines, a virus needs to be grown in human tissue. One way to do this is to use human cells. These cells must have special characteristics. They need to be strong enough to grow and replicate outside of the human body in labs over time. Cells with this ability can be found in some types of cancer. They can also be found in human fetuses. Scientists are able to collect these cells from cancerous tissue or a human fetus, then replicate it thousands of times over decades.

The moral objections to using vaccines produced using human tissue, especially those that are grown in cells from fetuses, are very strong for many people. The Catholic Church has even weighed in on the issue. It advises Catholics to use such vaccines in order to maintain the public health, but it also encourages people to work on developing alternatives that do not rely on human tissue to work.

vaccines. These communities are often linked by religious beliefs or cultural ideas that influence their medical decisions. Some medical professionals note these clusters can be dangerous. In these communities, outbreaks can travel quickly among unvaccinated people, leading to dangerous and even fatal outcomes.

One group of people who heavily influence the vaccine debate is found in a surprising place: Hollywood, California. Celebrities have taken on a prominent role in public debates about vaccines. Some of the most outspoken people have had a large impact on the way millions of people think about vaccine safety.

One of the most influential celebrities in this area is Jenny McCarthy. Following the publication of Wakefield's now-debunked paper linking autism to the MMR vaccine, McCarthy went public about her own son's autism and her suspicion it was caused by vaccines. McCarthy publicized her feelings on television, in magazines, and on the Internet.

Reality television personality Kristen Cavallari has repeatedly spoken out about how she will not vaccinate her children. Actor Alicia Silverstone echoes McCarthy's concerns about the medical establishment's "one-size-fits-all, shoot-'em up [vaccine] schedule."[4] Real-estate tycoon and television personality Donald Trump

CHANGING VIEWS

In the early 2000s, Jenny McCarthy warned parents of the potential dangers of vaccines. However, in recent years, her position has become more moderate. The following quotes reflect how her stance on vaccines has evolved over the years:

2010: "With so many kids with autism, the environment has to be to blame, and vaccines are an obvious culprit. Almost all kids get vaccines—injected toxins—very early in life, and our own government clearly acknowledges vaccines cause brain damage in certain vulnerable kids."[5]

2014: "I am not 'anti-vaccine.' This is not a change in my stance nor is it a new position that I have recently adopted. For years, I have repeatedly stated that I am, in fact, 'pro-vaccine' and for years I have been wrongly branded as 'anti-vaccine.'"[6]

has weighed in on the issue, suggesting that perhaps the "monster shots" of vaccines were linked to autism.[7]

While the people who object to vaccines are a small minority, they have a large voice in the media. Some of these individuals use their fame to spread their message. Scientific organizations such as the World Health Organization (WHO) and the CDC are forced to contend with the word of superstar celebrities, and they are often unable to get equal attention in the media. Because of this imbalance, the public may perceive both sides of the vaccine debate as being potentially valid. However, the scientific consensus surrounding vaccine safety is not affected by the opinions of celebrities.

CELEBRITY VACCINE ADVOCATES

Not all of Hollywood opposes vaccines. In fact, a large group of celebrities are outspoken activists who have worked with charities to help more children become vaccinated. Actors Amanda Peet, Keri Russell, and Jennifer Lopez have all spoken publicly about their support for different vaccines. Musician Mark Anthony has also added his voice to the pro-vaccine chorus.

Some celebrities even partner with health organizations to help spread the word about vaccines. Actor Jennifer Garner teamed up with the American Lung Association in 2007 to support the influenza vaccine. Another actor, Salma Hayek, became the spokeswoman for an initiative to vaccinate children in Africa and Asia against tetanus.

In the early 2000s, Jenny McCarthy, *right*, and Jim Carrey were among the most outspoken celebrity anti-vaccine advocates.

CHAPTER FIVE

MAKING
VACCINES

O nce a vaccine is released to the public, it can be administered to millions of people quickly. For example, in the year 2013 alone, approximately 112 million infants worldwide were given the vaccine for diphtheria, tetanus, and pertussis.[1] The large numbers of people who could be affected by a vaccine mean health officials take vaccine safety extremely seriously. Any potential side effects could be experienced by millions of people.

The goal of vaccine creators is to make an injection, nasal spray, or pill that mimics an infection inside the body without any of the harmful side effects of that disease. By doing this, the vaccine teaches the body's

The WHO and other international health agencies provide diphtheria, tetanus, and pertussis vaccines to children in impoverished nations, such as Liberia.

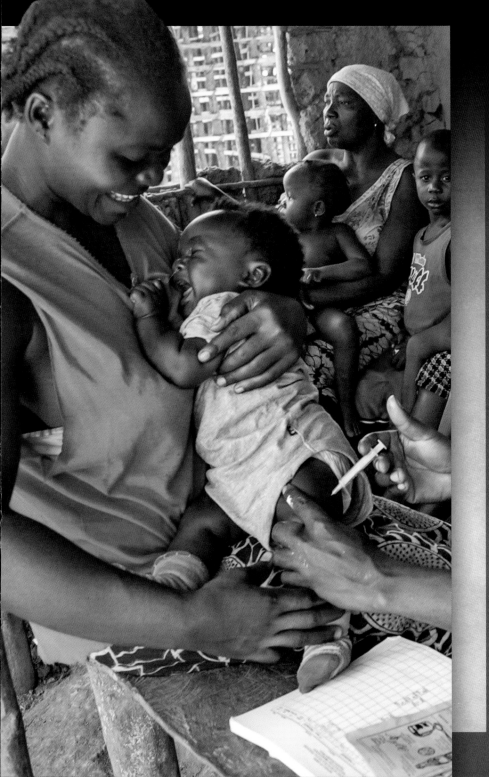

immune system to fight a disease so it will be prepared if it encounters the disease later. However, this can be very difficult to achieve. Scientists must strike a balance, stimulating the immune system without actually making the person ill.

MAKING A VACCINE

The process of creating a vaccine is long, painstaking, and often filled with setbacks. Vaccines are created in laboratories and are licensed by large medical organizations such as the FDA and the Center for Biological Evaluation and Research in the United States. Elsewhere, organizations such as the WHO monitor and recommend vaccines. Vaccine proponents argue the development process leads to safe vaccines, but anti-vaccine advocates worry the process can still result in oversights and errors that can lead to harmful consequences. They fear the vaccines are not tested for long enough periods of time and the testing is not thorough enough.

To start the process, scientists identify the antigens that can prevent a disease. Antigens used in vaccines can come from weakened or dead virus particles, weakened bacterial toxins, or substances that are very similar to virus particles. Once scientists identify the antigen, they grow it in a lab. Then they add substances that stabilize and preserve the antigen. They might also add substances to help enhance the immune system's response to the antigen. Finally, these substances are packaged in sterile, travel-safe containers for shipping to doctors around the world.

FEARS ABOUT HOW VACCINES ARE CREATED

Some people worry the way vaccines are created is dangerous. They do not feel comfortable with vaccines that include live or weakened fragments of a virus. They

SAFETY AT THE CDC

Much of the US research surrounding contagious disease and vaccine development happens inside the CDC. Scientists there often work with extremely dangerous and contagious diseases. In order to do this safely and without becoming infected, they must follow strict rules. The areas where scientists work with diseases are classified into different safety levels ranging from one to four. The increasing numbers, known as biosafety levels, involve more dangerous diseases that require additional precautions.

At biosafety level one, scientists work on lab tables or benches and wear lab coats, gloves, and protective eyewear as needed. The organisms they work with are considered to be minimally dangerous, such as the bacteria *E. coli.*

At biosafety level four, scientists work with diseases considered extremely dangerous and even fatal. Workers wear full-body airtight suits with their own air supply. An example of a virus found on this level is the Ebola virus.

worry these substances are toxic and could lead to serious illness. Others have strong objections to some of the substances scientists add to vaccines to make them last longer or stimulate the immune system. Some types of mercury, for example, have been added to many different types of vaccines as a preservative.

In the 1970s, people raised the alarm that mercury could be harmful when consumed, and therefore should not be included in a vaccine. Although scientists determined the amount of mercury included in vaccines was so small that it was not harmful, the FDA worked alongside drug manufacturers to remove the element from all vaccines intended for children younger than six years as a precautionary measure. The response showed some people that the government and drug companies cared about their

FORMALDEHYDE SAFETY

In 2011, the National Institutes of Health declared the chemical formaldehyde could cause cancer. This news was disturbing to many because formaldehyde is found in vaccines given to children. Some critics suggested the chemical caused childhood cancers.

Scientists rushed to reassure parents and other concerned people. They explained the amount of formaldehyde found in vaccines is extremely small. In fact, higher levels of formaldehyde are actually produced naturally by the human body. The chemical is important to the process of creating vaccines because it is used to inactivate live viruses, making them safe to include in injections, pills, or nasal sprays.

concerns, but others believed the FDA's action showed they were right to be worried.

TESTING VACCINES

Today, drug companies and scientists work hard to ensure the ingredients in vaccines are safe. Once a vaccine has been created, it must be thoroughly tested. The first tests usually do not involve humans. Instead, scientists test the way the vaccine affects cells in test tubes and petri dishes. After that, they may do testing on animals, such as mice or monkeys. They do this to try to predict how a human body will respond to the vaccine. Sometimes, scientists conduct

Many anti-vaccine advocates cite the presence of mercury in vaccines as a reason for rejecting immunization.

challenge studies on their animal test subjects. This means they vaccinate the animals, then intentionally expose them to the disease to see if they become infected. If these tests suggest the vaccine is safe and effective, it moves on to the next level of testing: clinical trials.

Clinical trials are an important part of vaccine testing. In Phase I clinical trials, a small group of adults receives the vaccine. This group is usually made up of 20 to 80 volunteers. In this stage, researchers confirm the vaccine is safe and look for any side effects. They also watch carefully to see how the human immune system responds to the vaccine. If the tested vaccine is intended for children, researchers start with adults and then gradually test younger and younger subjects.

ANIMAL TESTING CONTROVERSY

Many vaccines are tested on animals, such as mice and rats. Animal rights activists argue it is cruel to test vaccines on animals. They feel the test animals often experience discomfort, pain, and death. They also point out that test animals are usually raised in labs, and therefore have poor quality of life even before they become test subjects. These people often believe animals should not be used for vaccine testing, or any medical testing at all. Instead, they think scientists should use live human tissue, dead human bodies, and computer models in their tests.

Many scientists disagree. They feel test animals are extremely important to the development of new vaccines. They argue the best efforts are made to keep the animals comfortable. They say alternative tests using human tissue or computer programs do not work as well.

Phase II clinical trials involve a larger group of test subjects, usually hundreds of people. In this phase, researchers are still testing the vaccine for safety and immune system responses. But they are also studying the subjects to learn about the best dosages, timing, and method of administration.

If the vaccine successfully passes Phase II clinical trials, it moves on to Phase III. In this phase, tens of thousands of people receive the vaccine. Researchers are looking for any rare side effects that would not be likely to show up in the smaller test groups.

The final stage of vaccine development is getting a license. In the United States, the FDA gives licenses. Other health organizations license vaccines in other countries. This licensing step is critical to the process of ensuring vaccines are safely manufactured. Before issuing a license for the United States, inspectors from the FDA examine the factory where the vaccine is produced to make sure it is sterile and following the appropriate rules. They also test to make sure the vaccines doses being produced are consistent and do not contain foreign substances.

Not all vaccines are approved at the same time around the world. For example, a vaccine may be licensed in Europe months or years before it is licensed in the United States. This causes some distrust among anti-vaccine activists. They wonder why there is disagreement about the safety of a vaccine. However, pro-vaccine advocates explain this by pointing out different health organizations have different standards and procedures for approving drugs and vaccines.

Despite this thorough testing process, some people do not believe the safety of vaccines is fully established. They worry the long-term effects of some vaccines are

The process of developing, testing, licensing, and manufacturing vaccines is long and expensive.

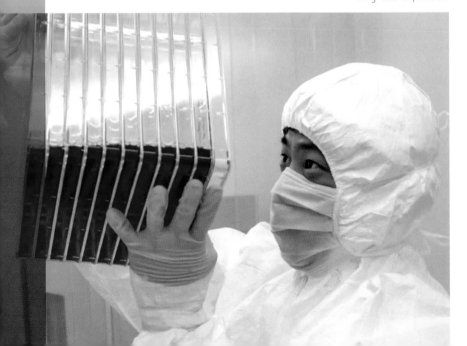

unknown. They also point to the fact that vaccine oversight is left to a small number of large organizations, such as the CDC and the FDA. They wonder whether these organizations are somehow profiting or benefiting from the use of vaccines. There is no evidence for this notion.

After a vaccine has been approved and licensed by the FDA, some drug companies choose to continue testing it. One reason they do this is to make sure the vaccine remains safe. They also do this to learn if their vaccine might have any other potential uses. They may discover that a vaccine developed for one disease works on another disease. This is beneficial for the drug companies, because it gives them the potential to make twice the profit from a single

A COVER-UP?

In 2014, news media outlets were abuzz with an inflammatory story about the CDC. It looked as though the health organization had covered up a study showing the MMR vaccine increased the risk for African-American males to develop autism by 340 percent.[2] Soon after the story appeared, it vanished. The disappearance made conspiracy theorists even more suspicious that the CDC was trying to squash the story.

The CDC responded quickly to the claims, noting the accusations came from a flawed interpretation of a study. The people behind the accusation had only looked at some parts of the study. They had made errors in analyzing the statistics. Though several news outlets published the CDC's response, many anti-vaccine advocates thought the incident cast doubt on the medical organization's credibility.

vaccine. This motivation raises red flags for some vaccine skeptics. They wonder if drug companies are simply looking to make money off of their vaccines, rather than contribute to the public's health.

DRUG COMPANIES AND THE MONEY MOTIVATION

The drug companies that make the majority of vaccines are sometimes referred to as Big Pharma. This is short for big pharmaceutical companies. They produce vaccines, drugs, and other health-care products. Many vaccine skeptics fear people working for Big Pharma are motivated by money rather than the goal of helping people. They point out some drug companies report tens of billions of dollars in profits each year.[3] Many US drug companies also receive funding from the US government to research and develop vaccines. This makes some people distrust both the drug companies and the government recommendations to vaccinate. They worry vaccines are part of a scheme to make profits and pay drug companies.

On the other side of the debate, many vaccine advocates point out Big Pharma's profits are misleading.

MORE TO THE STORY

ROTAVIRUS VACCINES

Rotavirus is a common contagious virus that causes diarrhea, vomiting, and painful cramps. In 1998, the FDA approved the first rotavirus vaccine, RotaShield. Soon after the approval, a small number of children who had received the vaccine developed a rare intestinal obstruction. The CDC investigated and determined the vaccine increased a child's risk of developing the bowel obstruction by one to two cases for every 10,000 children vaccinated. Though this number was very small, the CDC found it serious enough to suspend the use of the RotaShield vaccine.[4]

It would take another eight years for the next rotavirus vaccine to enter the market. In 2006, the FDA approved the vaccine RotaTeq. Two years later came another vaccine, Rotarix. Both of these vaccines were studied very carefully to determine whether they increased a child's chances of developing bowel problems. They were both found to be safe.

Again, however, this success did not last long. In 2010, an independent team of scientists discovered Rotarix contained DNA from a pig virus. Though the vaccine was found to be safe for humans, the FDA chose to act cautiously and recommend doctors stop using it. This incident caused many people to again question the safety of vaccines.

They acknowledge that while these companies make a lot of money, vaccines make up a very small portion of their total income. The majority of their profits come from other drugs or health-care products. Vaccine advocates also point out that drug companies spend enormous amounts of money researching, testing, and distributing their products. Much of the money they make on existing vaccines goes back into testing and producing new vaccines.

A LENGTHY PROCESS

The process of creating, testing, and seeking licensure for a vaccine typically takes between 10 and 15 years. This means it is very difficult for drug companies to quickly respond to a new contagious disease. However, new diseases and variations on old diseases are constantly appearing. Scientists must work to be as prepared as possible to confront them.

When H1N1 swept across the world in 2009, scientists worked with the CDC at a breakneck pace to create a vaccine as quickly as possible. The history of deadly influenza pandemics drove this rapid development.

Pharmaceutical companies around the world rapidly developed and manufactured an H1N1 vaccine in 2009.

FROM THE
HEADLINES

EBOLA AND THE RACE FOR A VACCINE

Ebola is a deadly disease. People suffering from it experience a variety of symptoms, ranging from headache and diarrhea to bleeding to organ failure. A large proportion of the people who catch Ebola die from it.

The year 2014 saw the largest outbreak of the Ebola virus in history. It swept across multiple countries in West Africa. A few cases reached Europe and the United States. The outbreak claimed thousands of lives.

At the beginning of the outbreak, US government officials and hospital administrators rushed to develop new safety procedures to prevent sick people from spreading Ebola. States such as New York and New Jersey forced healthy medical workers who had been exposed to the disease into strict quarantines, just to be sure they could not spread the disease. Many people felt this extreme response was unnecessary. They cautioned it only added to the Ebola panic.

In other areas of the United States, health-care administrators faced harsh criticism for not taking enough precautions against the contagious disease. Two nurses in Dallas, Texas, contracted Ebola after caring for a sick patient who died from the disease. Both nurses made full recoveries. One later sued her employers at

Experimental Ebola vaccines underwent
early testing in October 2014.

the hospital, claiming they did not do enough to protect her from the disease.

At the beginning of the outbreak, drug companies rushed to respond. Vaccines went into development at drug companies and national health organizations in the United States and Canada. Researchers are hopeful at least one of these vaccines may prevent future outbreaks of the scope and magnitude of the 2014 epidemic.

For vaccines to be effective, patients must trust doctors, drug companies, and safety regulations enough to actually use them.

1918 pandemic killed as many as 40 million people.[5]

Because H1N1 was a strain of influenza, scientists were able

to use work they had done on other types of influenza to

get started. After speeding up nearly every stage of the

process, they were successful. By December 2009, 100

million doses of the H1N1 vaccine became available for hospitals and clinics to order.[6]

Each time a parent watches his or her child receive a vaccination, he or she must trust the vaccine is safe, tested, and reliable. This involves trust for the doctor, the drug companies that produced the vaccine, and the health organization that licensed it. For some people, this is easy. They trust the science behind vaccines is sound, and they believe health organizations are trying to save lives through vaccination. For others, this trust is more difficult. They worry mistakes could have happened or risks could have been ignored. For people who mistrust their physicians, health organizations, drug companies, or even governments, vaccines can be difficult to accept.

CHAPTER SIX

NEW VACCINES,
NEW WORRIES

Since the year 2000, there have been amazing developments in the creation, production, and administration of vaccines. Scientists have knocked down obstacles that stood in the way of vaccine research in the past. Discoveries about the way viruses behave, combined with advanced technology, have allowed scientists to explore innovative techniques for preventing the spread of disease.

Dr. Nancy Sullivan is the chief researcher at the National Institute of Allergy and Infectious Diseases vaccine research lab in Bethesda, Maryland.

NASAL SPRAYS

In 2003, scientists introduced an influenza vaccine that would appeal to people who disliked injections. This new vaccine was instead delivered via a nasal spray. The CDC reported the nasal flu spray could reduce a person's chances of getting influenza by 92 percent.[1] Unlike the injectable influenza vaccine, which was made from a dead virus, this new vaccine used a weakened live flu virus. Scientists chose to use a live virus because of the way it interacted with the immune system. They carefully engineered a version of the flu virus that was very weak and could survive only at low temperatures. This meant after it had been inhaled into warm

MICRONEEDLE PATCHES

Most vaccines are delivered via a needle injection into the muscle or deep layers of skin. However, this method is not perfect. It uses large amounts of vaccine fluid, and it exposes health-care workers to possible injuries, such as being stuck by a needle. It may also scare away patients afraid of needles.

Scientists have been exploring a new option: microneedle patches. These adhesive patches are proving to be easy, effective ways to deliver vaccines. The underside of the patch is covered with 100 small, hair-like needles.[2] Drug companies can coat the underside of these patches with a small amount of vaccine. Then, health care workers can simply apply them to a patient's body like a sticker. In 2015, microneedle patches were undergoing testing and were not yet available to the public.

human lungs, it activated the immune system but could not reproduce and cause the flu.

Not everyone could choose the nasal spray vaccine, however. Some groups of people were excluded from using it. Children who were younger than two years and children with asthma were advised not to use the nasal mist because it could increase their risk of breathing problems.

Just as with many other vaccines, the nasal mist flu vaccine was met with criticism and doubt by many. Some of the biggest objections against the new sprayed vaccine were related to its ingredients. Religious groups have

Tens of millions of nasal flu spray vaccinations have been given since their introduction in 2003.

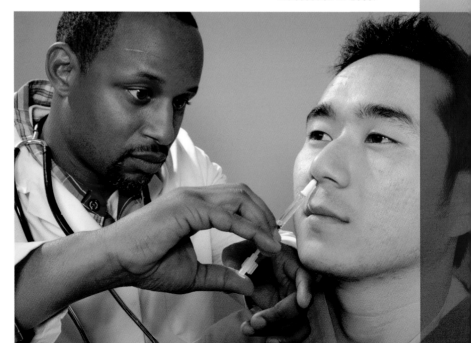

protested the fact that the vaccine contains pork proteins. Some religions have restrictions against consuming pork, so some of their followers chose to avoid the vaccine.

Another ingredient in the vaccine that has some people hesitant is monosodium glutamate (MSG). This food additive, often found in salad dressings and diet foods, is used to stabilize the vaccine. Many people who eat MSG have reported negative symptoms, such as headache, weakness, and fatigue. A movement in the 1960s even led to MSG being banned from baby foods in the United States. However, controlled studies have been unable to replicate the negative symptoms. US health authorities have since recognized MSG as a safe food additive. The amount of MSG in vaccines is a tiny fraction of the amount found in common foods.

VACCINATING AGAINST NEW DISEASES

One area of rapid growth is the development of vaccines against new diseases, including types of cancer. Cancer is a group of diseases, rather than a single disease, and different cancers can cause a wide range of effects. Scientists know some lifestyle choices, such as not

smoking and eating a healthy diet, can reduce the chances
of developing some cancers. But they also recognize that
some cancers are inherited. This means they are passed
from one generation to another. Developing a vaccine
against a particular cancer seemed like a difficult or even
impossible task.

However, in the 1980s, German scientists made
an important discovery. They found the human
papillomavirus (HPV) could cause cervical cancer in
women. Researchers realized if a vaccine could be made
against this virus, cases of cervical cancer could be
prevented. It took more than two decades of research

In November 2014, President Barack Obama awarded the National Medal of
Science to the researchers who helped develop the HPV vaccine.

and testing, but in 2006, health organizations in several countries, including the FDA in the United States, licensed a vaccine for HPV. This was a major step in vaccine history. For the first time, scientists were able to prevent cancer through vaccination.

PROBLEMS WITH THE HPV VACCINE

While many greeted the news about a cancer vaccine with excitement, others reacted with fear and hesitation. HPV is often spread through sexual activity. Some people worried vaccinating teens against HPV would encourage them to engage in risky sexual behavior. Studies later proved that this was not true. Teens who had received the HPV vaccine did not participate in riskier sexual behavior than those who had not. Other skeptics objected to the HPV vaccine because of safety concerns. They worried about the ingredients in the vaccine and the potential side effects.

"WELL, I WILL TELL YOU THAT I HAD A MOTHER LAST NIGHT COME UP TO ME HERE IN TAMPA, FLORIDA, AFTER THE DEBATE. . . . SHE TOLD ME THAT HER LITTLE DAUGHTER TOOK THAT [HPV] VACCINE, THAT INJECTION, AND SHE SUFFERED FROM MENTAL RETARDATION THEREAFTER. IT CAN HAVE VERY DANGEROUS SIDE EFFECTS."[3]

—POLITICIAN MICHELE BACHMANN

After the first few years of use, studies began being published detailing the HPV vaccine's effects. More than 23 million doses of the vaccine were given between 2006 and 2008.[4] Women who received the vaccine saw greatly reduced rates of cervical cancer. Vaccine advocates celebrated this news. They pointed to the fact that very few negative side effects had been experienced.

Anti-vaccine proponents, on the other hand, looked at the CDC's data differently. They noted more than 12,000 reports of negative side effects from the vaccine were made to VAERS. While most of these reports were related to mild side effects, there were 32 reports of people who had died after receiving the vaccine.[5] The CDC stressed in its report that these deaths were not caused by the vaccine.

HPV VACCINE AND SIDE EFFECTS

The most popular HPV vaccine is called Gardasil. Soon after Gardasil entered doctors' offices, parents and teens began complaining about the vaccine's side effects. Some complaints were related to mild symptoms, such as headaches or nausea. Others seemed to be more severe. A Japanese news article claimed the vaccine caused infertility. Some patients even told stories of seizures and temporary vision loss.

Many physicians cautioned patients to be critical of these stories. They reminded patients it was unlikely these symptoms were actually caused by the vaccine. As public health writer Robyn Carlyle put it, "If someone eats a peanut butter sandwich and then drives to work and gets into a car accident, does that mean that peanut butter sandwiches cause car crashes? Of course not."[6]

FROM THE
HEADLINES

POLITICIANS AND VACCINES

Choosing whether to vaccinate is a personal medical decision. Yet many politicians have weighed in on the vaccine debate. This is because many schools and workplaces have policies that require vaccinations. Some people feel as though these policies are an infringement on their personal freedoms. They believe they should be able to make their own choices about whether to have themselves or their children vaccinated.

US senator Rand Paul of Kentucky is one politician who has gotten involved in the vaccine debate. He believes the decision whether or not to vaccinate should be left up to individuals. "I'm not anti-vaccine at all," he said in an interview, "but most of them ought to be voluntary."[7] In a subsequent interview, Rand went on to say, "I have heard of many tragic cases of walking, talking, normal children who wound up with profound mental disorders after vaccines."[8] His statement is not supported by evidence, yet it resonated with anti-vaccination proponents.

Other politicians have weighed in on the other side of the debate. In 2015, Hillary Clinton tweeted "The science is clear: The earth is round, the sky is blue, and #vaccineswork. Let's protect all our kids. #GrandmothersKnowBest."[9]

Rand Paul is one of several politicians who have expressed doubts about vaccine safety.

But some anti-vaccine activists did not believe this. They felt the CDC and others in the medical field were intentionally misleading the public about these deaths. These skeptics thought the CDC and other health organizations were working with drug companies to make money off the vaccines. They worried the girls had died as a result of a vaccine that was produced simply to make money for Big Pharma.

A RANGE OF RESPONSES

This constant evolution of vaccine science means some parents of young children must make new vaccine decisions every time they visit the doctor. One way people respond to new vaccines is to opt out entirely. Anti-vaccine activists often choose this route. They do not receive any vaccinations, regardless of how long they have been in use. Others choose a middle ground. They choose to only get vaccines that have been used for many years. Some people choose to vaccinate only against diseases they feel personally worried about. People who are pro-vaccine often choose to receive all of the vaccinations on the schedule recommended by the FDA, CDC, or WHO. Others, worried about safety or side effects, choose to follow an alternative vaccine schedule.

Alternative vaccine schedules were first suggested by physician Robert Sears. He was concerned about the aluminum additive found in many vaccines, though the evidence shows this additive is harmless in small amounts. He believed that in order to prevent overwhelming a child's body with aluminum, doctors should give children fewer shots at a time. He also suggested doctors not administer shots containing multiple vaccines. He felt these steps would allow children's bodies to better cope with the immune system's response to vaccines.

WHO IS DR. SEARS?

Dr. Sears is one of the leading voices in the vaccine debate. The Harvard-educated physician is not an outright anti-vaccine advocate. He acknowledges that vaccines are effective. However, he is not entirely pro-vaccine, either. Rather, he falls into a middle group in the vaccine debate. Sears believes parents and patients should be concerned about vaccines and their ingredients and choose the ones they believe are right for their family.

In 2007, Sears wrote, "Vaccines have played a tremendous role in eliminating or limiting the diseases in our country." But he reminded readers that parents should do their own research when deciding "whether or not to vaccinate, and how to vaccinate in the safest manner possible."[8]

Sears is well-known for questioning the safety of some additives in vaccines. One additive he frequently mentions is aluminum. Though many studies have found aluminum to be safe in vaccines, Sears continues to advocate that parents choose vaccines that do not include aluminum or follow an alternative vaccine schedule to avoid overloading young children's immune systems. Pro-vaccine advocates have criticized him for encouraging parents to delay vaccination and leave their children vulnerable to deadly diseases.

Alternative vaccine schedules are popular among groups of parents who are worried about the side effects of vaccines. However, mainstream physicians do not endorse them. The American Academy of Pediatrics (AAP) opposes alternative vaccine schedules. The chair of the AAP's section on infectious diseases, Margaret Fisher, reminds parents, "When you delay vaccines, you leave children unprotected against dangerous diseases at the time when they're most vulnerable."[11]

By 2015, the vaccine schedule for US children included more than a dozen vaccines. Some people think so many shots could be harmful, but the evidence does not support that opinion.

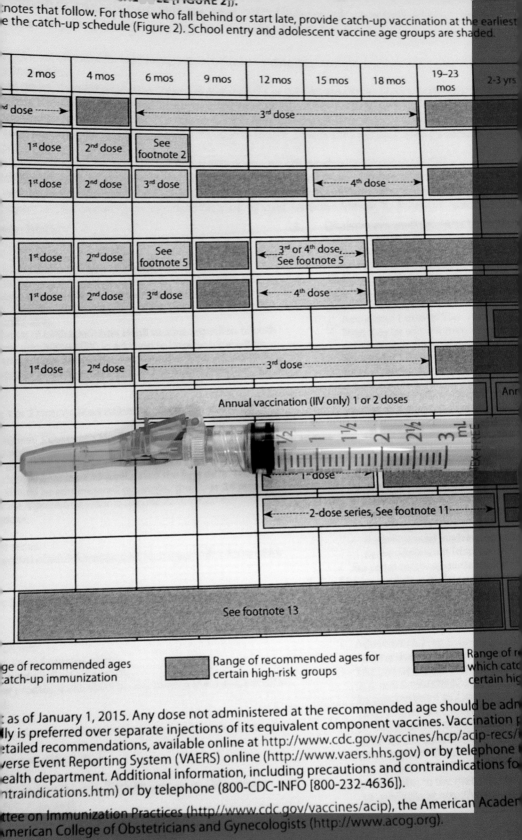

2 mos	4 mos	6 mos	9 mos	12 mos	15 mos	18 mos	19–23 mos	2-3 yrs
nd dose ┄┄┄►		◄┄┄┄┄┄┄┄┄┄ 3rd dose ┄┄┄┄┄┄┄┄┄┄►						
1st dose	2nd dose	See footnote 2						
1st dose	2nd dose	3rd dose			◄┄┄┄┄ 4th dose ┄┄┄┄►			
1st dose	2nd dose	See footnote 5		◄┄┄ 3rd or 4th dose, ┄┄► See footnote 5				
1st dose	2nd dose	3rd dose		◄┄┄┄ 4th dose ┄┄┄┄►				
1st dose	2nd dose	◄┄┄┄┄┄┄┄┄┄┄ 3rd dose ┄┄┄┄┄┄┄┄┄┄┄►						
			Annual vaccination (IIV only) 1 or 2 doses					Anr
				1 dose ┄┄►				
				◄┄┄┄┄┄ 2-dose series, See footnote 11 ┄┄┄┄┄┄►				
See footnote 13								

ge of recommended ages
catch-up immunization

Range of recommended ages for
certain high-risk groups

Range of re
which catc
certain hig

: as of January 1, 2015. Any dose not administered at the recommended age should be adm
ly is preferred over separate injections of its equivalent component vaccines. Vaccination p
etailed recommendations, available online at http://www.cdc.gov/vaccines/hcp/acip-recs/
verse Event Reporting System (VAERS) online (http://www.vaers.hhs.gov) or by telephone
ealth department. Additional information, including precautions and contraindications fo
ntraindications.htm) or by telephone (800-CDC-INFO [800-232-4636]).

ttee on Immunization Practices (http//www.cdc.gov/vaccines/acip), the American Acader
American College of Obstetricians and Gynecologists (http://www.acog.org).

CHAPTER SEVEN

THE GLOBAL
IMPACT OF
VACCINES

O ne reason the vaccine debate is such a hot topic is that the diseases affect people living around the entire world. While some vaccines are created to combat diseases found in small areas of the world, others are intended for the global population. This means health organizations distribute hundreds of millions of vaccines each year.

THE WORLD'S UNVACCINATED CHILDREN

Organizations such as the WHO work hard to spread vaccines around the entire globe, focusing especially on poor and rural areas. People living in these places

International vaccine assistance is especially important in the aftermath of major disasters, such as the 2010 Haiti earthquake.

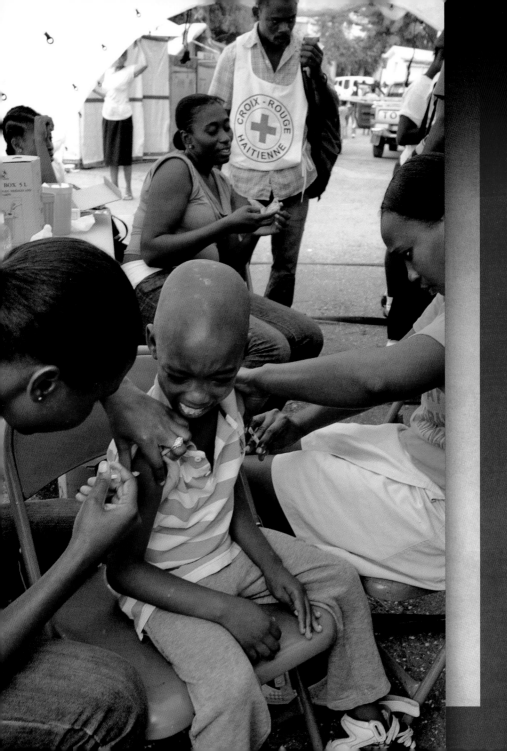

often lack access to medical care and suffer from more vaccine-preventable diseases. However, despite their efforts, many children remain unvaccinated. In 2007, approximately 20 percent of children worldwide did not get the vaccines recommended for their first year of life.[1] This occurs for many different reasons. Children in rural areas may lack access to modern health care. Some rural communities are uneducated about health-care recommendations. Others are not vaccinated because their families have made the decision to avoid vaccinations.

The WHO sees the gap in immunized children as a big problem. It estimates approximately 1 million children die each year as a result of vaccine-preventable diseases.[2]

Some vaccine skeptics interpret things differently.

FOOD ALLERGIES AND VACCINES

In the last few decades, vaccines have become more and more prevalent around the world. During that same period of time, doctors have seen a sharp increase in the number of children with allergies, such as asthma and eczema. Many vaccine skeptics wondered if the vaccines were causing the allergies.

Most of the studies conducted on this topic show vaccinations do not affect allergy rates in children. However, one study seemed to show a connection. It found that a small group of children who received fewer vaccines reported fewer allergies. However, the authors of the study explained these children attended the doctor less frequently in general. Therefore, their true allergy rates may have been similar, but they did not go to the doctor to report them.

MORE TO THE STORY

A VACCINE'S JOURNEY

When a vaccine is ready for use, it needs to be safely transported from the lab where it was created. This often means it must be packaged in individual doses so health-care workers can easily administer it to patients. It must also be carefully sealed so it is not contaminated during its journey. Finally, many vaccines need to be kept at a precise temperature to prevent them from spoiling during their journey. This last requirement can be difficult during cross-country or interstate journeys. And it can be nearly impossible for vaccines that need to travel across the globe to extremely rural areas or war-torn nations.

In the past, drug companies have relied on small refrigerators powered by batteries, propane gas, and even solar power. But these often fail. If the vaccines inside a refrigerator become too warm, they are spoiled and must be discarded. This amount of waste was infuriating for both drug companies and the doctors who were trying to provide vaccinations.

A new invention may make vaccines' global journeys a bit easier. It is a cooler that is so well insulated it can keep a vaccine at the right temperature for more than a month using only ice. It even maintains its temperature after being opened and shut many times. This is extremely important, since health-care workers need to be able to reach in and get one vaccine at a time without raising the temperature and ruining the whole batch.

They look at the number of unvaccinated children living around the world as evidence vaccines are not necessary. They point out many people living in these unvaccinated communities have developed natural immunity to the diseases through being exposed to sick people. They emphasize natural immunity is often stronger than the immunity developed from vaccines. Vaccine proponents note that though some people will gain stronger immunity, those with weaker immune systems may die from these diseases.

Most of the unvaccinated people in the world are found in Africa and Asia. This means those continents are home to many outbreaks of diseases scientists say are preventable. Because global travel is so easy and common, these disease outbreaks can quickly spread to communities around the world. For example, in March 2015, officials at Singapore's Ministry of Health scrambled to contact passengers on two China Airlines flights after realizing a flight attendant had the disease rubella. Officials feared the flight attendant could have exposed up to 1,500 people to the disease.[3] However, because many people in Singapore are vaccinated against rubella, a major outbreak did not occur.

VACCINE COSTS

All of the efforts to prevent the spread of disease add up to considerable financial costs. For example, the US government has spent more than $100 million fighting the outbreak of Ebola alone.[4] This money is spent on everything ranging from the salaries of scientists researching the disease to the cost of sending health-care workers to Africa to care for ill patients.

Some anti-vaccine advocates wonder if the money spent on vaccines could be better used elsewhere. As multiple large drug companies develop more and more vaccines, the price for each

VACCINES OR COINCIDENCE?

In the last 50 years, the number of deaths from contagious diseases has plummeted. Pro-vaccine advocates see this as evidence that vaccines are effective ways to prevent disease. Vaccine skeptics, on the other hand, see the picture differently.

Anti-vaccine advocates sometimes point out the fact that many changes occurred in society at the same time vaccines became more common. People learned about how better hygiene can prevent illness, how nutrition contributes to overall health, and how to make public water systems cleaner and more reliable. These advocates believe these changes, rather than vaccines, led to a drop in disease rates. Their position runs counter to the evidence, which shows a clear connection between vaccination and death rates from a wide variety of diseases.

Doctors Without Borders held a protest outside the headquarters of Pfizer in April 2015, calling for cheaper vaccines.

vaccine is rising. Some companies earn large profits from vaccines. For example, two drug companies, Pfizer and GlaxoSmithKline, have made more than $19 billion in sales of just one type of vaccine.[5] This type of financial gain makes some feel uneasy. The group Doctors Without Borders, which provides medical services in poor areas, has called for lower vaccine prices. A leading member of the organization notes, "The price to fully vaccinate a child is 68 times more expensive than it was just over a decade ago."[6]

IS IT WORTH THE COST?

Organizations such as the WHO stress that the cost of vaccines is much less than the cost of treating people who are suffering from a disease. They note the ten-year campaign to rid the world of the smallpox virus was expensive, costing approximately $100 million. However, they also point out they believe it has saved approximately $1.3 billion per year in smallpox treatment and prevention costs ever since.[7]

Some vaccine skeptics do not agree with the WHO's claims. They believe smallpox was already naturally becoming less common when the vaccine was created. They believe it was a coincidence the smallpox disease was eradicated after the smallpox vaccine was developed. These groups argue the money from smallpox vaccination

BILL GATES AND VACCINES

Microsoft founder Bill Gates and his wife, Melinda, are one of the wealthiest couples in the world. But that does not stop them from trekking to rugged, remote corners of the globe to encourage vaccination.

Their charity, the Bill and Melinda Gates Foundation, has lofty goals. It hopes to prevent more than 11 million deaths and 264 million illnesses by 2020 by increasing the number of vaccinated children around the globe.[8]

This vaccination mission is not cheap. In 2007, the Bill and Melinda Gates foundation invested $200 million in a project that hopes to wipe out polio. While this number might seem large, it was just the beginning. In 2010, the foundation pledged an additional $10 billion to support a decade of research into vaccines.[9]

FUNDING FOR VACCINE SKEPTICS

Anti-vaccination organizations work hard to get their message across to the public. From billboards to commercials, their efforts add up to a hefty price tag. Funding these efforts are a few wealthy families, businesses, and individuals that sympathize with anti-vaccine views.

The Dwoskin Family Foundation, for example, contributed nearly $1 million between 2011 and 2013 to anti-vaccine research.[11] It also helped fund the anti-vaccine documentary *The Greater Good*. And it gave money to one of the biggest anti-vaccine organizations, the National Vaccine Information Center.

could have gone into other treatments. This position is unsupported by the evidence.

The financial element of the vaccine debate is becoming increasingly important as many global powers struggle with poor economies. In 2010, it cost approximately $18 to fully vaccinate a child against contagious diseases. Experts warned this number was rising quickly. The United Nations Children's Rights & Emergency Relief Organization (UNICEF) predicts the cost could soon rise to $30 per child.[10] These costs reflect the new, expensive technologies used in vaccine development and delivery. As vaccines grow more expensive, the debate over safety and effectiveness is likely to continue.

Some people distrust the pharmaceutical industry, nicknamed Big Pharma by protesters, saying it seeks only profits.

PHARMA'$
WHEEL OF FORTUNE
WHICHEVER WAY YOU $PIN IT,
PHARMA WIN$
PHARMA:
BRING VACCINE
PRICE$ DOWN
SO MORE KID
CAN BE VACCINAT

THE FUTURE OF
THE VACCINE DEBATE

Much of the vaccine debate centers around questions of personal freedom. Pro-vaccine advocates feel that everyone should be required to vaccinate their children. They argue that by not getting vaccinated, people reduce the effectiveness of herd immunity, endangering the lives of those who cannot get vaccinated for medical reasons. Others feel they should not be required to accept any health-care decision that was made for them. They feel as though mandatory vaccinations represent a threat to their personal rights.

In April 2015, people protested California Senate Bill 277, which makes it harder to get exempted from vaccine requirements in public schools.

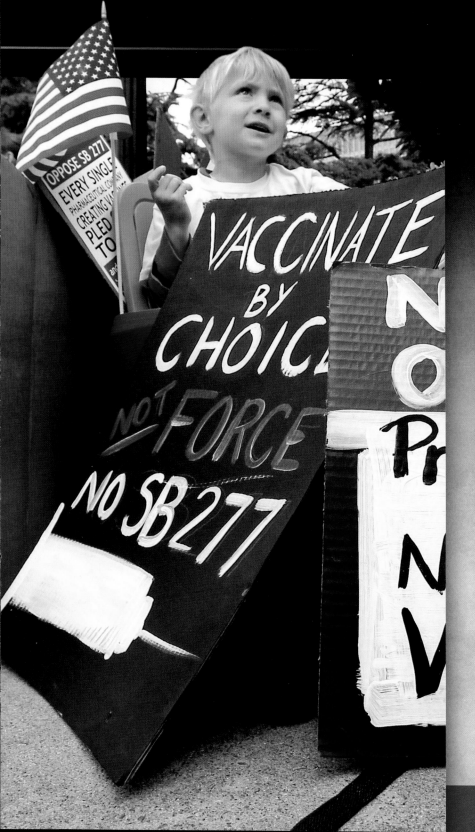

NO SHOTS, NO SCHOOL

The US government urges all families to vaccinate their children according to the standard vaccination schedule. In fact, all 50 states have laws requiring children to be immunized against some diseases before they can enter schools. These laws are explained as ways to keep the general public safe. Schools are small, concentrated areas full of people, meaning any infection could quickly spread and endanger many children.

However, these vaccine requirements leave room for exceptions. All 50 states allow exemptions for medical reasons. This means parents can opt out of vaccinating their children if they have a medical reason that makes the vaccine inappropriate or dangerous for their child. These medical exemptions are noncontroversial.

Almost all states also have exemptions for people with religious objections to vaccines. These exemptions allow people who do not believe in eating pork, for example, to opt out of a vaccine including pork proteins. The only states that do not allow people to use religion as a reason for not getting vaccinated are Mississippi and West Virginia.

CONTROVERSIAL EXEMPTIONS

Recently, new types of vaccine exemptions have emerged. These are often called nonmedical exemptions (NMEs). These exemptions allow people who do not have medical or religious reasons to avoid vaccines to still refuse them. People who worry about the side effects of vaccines or who feel vaccines are not necessary can claim a personal belief exemption to opt out of them.

Many people who protest mandatory vaccinations frame the issue as a matter of personal freedom.

In 2015, 19 states allowed these NMEs.[1] In these states, unvaccinated children can still attend school. Anti-vaccination organizations worked hard to get these exemptions written into the law. For many vaccine skeptics, the laws allowing NMEs are extremely important. They reflect the fact that not all Americans want to get vaccines. And they also allow the children of vaccine skeptics to receive the education other children have access to.

Some pro-vaccine lawmakers are fighting back against NMEs. In California, for example, a new law requires parents to meet with a physician before making the decision to opt out of vaccines for personal beliefs. They must be informed of the potential risks to which they are exposing their children. Some say this law has already resulted in an

DISEASE PARTIES

As the Disney measles outbreak of 2015 began winding down, reports of a new phenomenon emerged. People in California supposedly began hosting "measles parties," events hosted by families in which at least one person has the measles. The point of these parties is to expose others to the disease so they can develop a natural immunity to it. Similar parties had been held in the past for the disease chicken pox.

While no measles parties were ever confirmed, the very idea of them made news around the globe. Health officials and physicians warned families not to attend measles parties. "It's the worst idea I've heard in a long time," said one San Francisco physician. "Measles kills people, and I can't believe anyone would send their child to a party knowing that."[2]

increase in the number of vaccinated children in California. In 2014, for the first time since 2009, California saw a rise in the percentage of kindergarteners getting vaccines. Many people who favor vaccines saw this as a huge victory. After all, California has become a center of vaccine resistance in the United States. However, some point out the fact that the increase was extremely small: from 90.2 percent to 90.4 percent.[3] They note this change is so small it does not represent any larger change in opinions about vaccines.

A MURKY FUTURE

The future of the vaccine debate remains murky. It can often seem as though everything about vaccines invites argument. In fact, experts cannot even agree about the debate itself: is it slowing down or just getting started? A December 2014 headline from the *Los Angeles Times* declared, "Finally, the Anti-Vaccine Movement is Losing Steam."[4] However, just two months later, a headline from the *Houston Chronicle* reflected the opposite view: "Amid Measles Outbreaks, Non-Vaccination Movement Grows."[5] The exact state of the debate is difficult to interpret.

BIOTERRORISM

One surprising element of the vaccine debate has to do with bioterrorism, the threat that terrorists might use deadly viruses to kill huge numbers of people. In 2001, the US government simulated a secret biological attack with the code name Dark Winter. In this simulation, they realized a release of the smallpox virus onto US soil could have deadly consequences. There were not enough doses of the vaccine available to stop the disease. As a result of this simulation, millions of additional smallpox vaccinations were added to the US government's vaccine storage.

"TO RELY ON THE DRUG COMPANIES FOR UNBIASED EVALUATIONS OF THEIR PRODUCTS MAKES ABOUT AS MUCH SENSE AS RELYING ON BEER COMPANIES TO TEACH US ABOUT ALCOHOLISM."[6]

—DR. MARCIA ANGELL, FORMER EDITOR OF THE *NEW ENGLAND JOURNAL OF MEDICINE*

As new vaccines enter the market, new debates will likely follow. The ingredients, delivery methods, and reasons for vaccinations are all topics that have caused debate in the past.

THE CHANGING ROLE OF DRUG COMPANIES

Drug companies manufacture the vaccines used around the world. Because of this, they have an important role in the vaccine debate. Patients need to trust the drug companies are producing safe, effective vaccines at a reasonable price. Both pro- and anti-vaccine groups closely monitor these companies.

In 2011, the prices for some vaccines were getting very high. It was hard for nonprofit health organizations and

The production of vaccines is closely monitored to ensure safety.

governmental organizations to afford to buy them. Some

people worried these prices would stop people from being

vaccinated. In an attempt to shed light on vaccine pricing,

the global health organization

UNICEF made the prices for

some drug companies' vaccines

public. As the public saw the

price differences—varying

between companies by as much

as 40 percent for the same

vaccine—they put pressure

on the drug companies to

change.[7] Within days, some

drug companies responded,

drastically reducing their prices.

While this recent interaction

between drug companies and

health organizations suggests

cooperation, this is not always

the case. Drug companies are,

after all, corporations trying to

make a profit. They set their

THE SUPREME COURT PROTECTS DRUG COMPANIES

In 2011, the US Supreme Court ruled a family could not sue a drug company for vaccine-related injuries. The lawsuit, *Bruesewitz v. Wyeth*, was a landmark case. It involved a family whose infant suffered serious health problems after being vaccinated. They had tried to sue the drug company that made the vaccine for the problems their adult daughter continued to endure.

Supreme Court Justice Antonin Scalia commented on the ruling, noting that when vaccines are properly created, tested, and accompanied by "proper directions and warnings," then lawsuits should not be allowed.[8] Instead, a separate vaccine court set up by the US Congress in 1986 makes rulings on these issues. The Supreme Court's decision emphasizes the idea vaccines are safe and well tested. It also highlights that parents choosing to vaccinate their children should be aware of the potential risks and side effects they may cause.

UNICEF workers are among those on the front lines of the fight against diseases worldwide.

prices in order to make money and pay their employees. As new vaccines are created and distributed in the future, drug companies and health organizations will need to continue to work together.

AN ONGOING DEBATE

The vaccine debate is not just a disagreement between people who want to vaccinate their children and people who do not. It involves teams of scientists, global health organizations, multibillion-dollar drug companies, government leaders, celebrities, parents, and billions of children living around the world.

ARE DRUG COMPANIES SHARING THE WHOLE TRUTH?

Many people feel they cannot trust drug companies. In a recent survey, only 32 percent of people across the globe report they felt drug companies "act with integrity."[9] One reason people report a negative opinion of drug companies is the high prices of medicines. The profits reported by drug companies added to their suspicions.

Another reason for distrust of drug companies is that people feel there is a lack of communication with the public about the harmful effects of some drugs. They fear drug companies are either omitting or downplaying the harmful effects of different vaccines. This is an important issue when it comes to the vaccine debate. A distrust of drug companies has fueled the vaccine skeptics' fight.

The key issues at the heart of the vaccine debate are issues of trust in doctors and the medical establishment and the tension between personal freedoms and public safety. The science of vaccine safety is largely settled, but political debates over vaccines are poised to continue for years to come.

Vaccination remained a major subject of heated debate in the early decades of the 2000s.

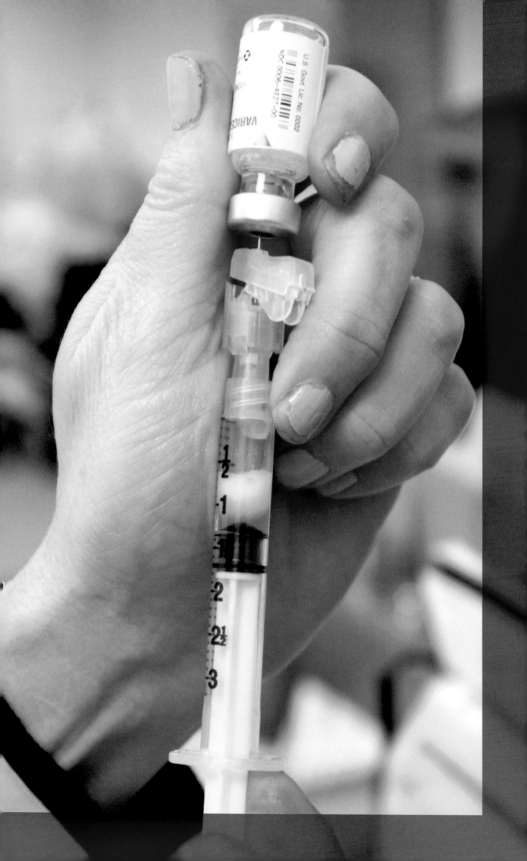

ESSENTIAL
FACTS

MAJOR EVENTS

- In 1998, Andrew Wakefield publishes a study that links the MMR vaccine to autism. His findings are later disproven.

- In the 1980s, German scientists discover the human papillomavirus (HPV) can cause cervical cancer. The finding leads to the development of an HPV vaccine that could effectively prevent cancer.

- From December 2014 to February 2015, a measles outbreak sweeps through southern California and spreads throughout the nation. The outbreak is blamed on people who had chosen to reject vaccination.

KEY PLAYERS

- Andrew Wakefield's study connecting vaccines to autism helps trigger a resurgence in vaccine opposition in the late 1990s.

- Jenny McCarthy has been one of the most outspoken celebrities linked to anti-vaccine activism.

- Dr. Robert Sears promotes an alternative vaccination schedule.

- Bill and Melinda Gates have pledged billions of dollars to vaccination programs around the world.

IMPACT ON SOCIETY

Vaccine controversies have been around since the introduction of vaccines. Questions of safety and effectiveness surrounded vaccines, but the dramatic drop in disease rates during the 1900s reduced the opposition to them. In the late 1900s and early 2000s, new controversies emerged about supposed safety concerns. Many people and organizations cited personal freedom as a reason for getting exemptions from mandatory vaccinations.

QUOTE

"There is every reason to get vaccinated—there aren't reasons to not."

—*President Barack Obama*

GLOSSARY

ANTIBODY
A protein the body produces to destroy bacteria or viruses that cause diseases.

ANTIGEN
Part of an infectious bacteria or virus to which the body's immune system responds.

CANCER
A group of diseases caused when cells divide rapidly and in an uncontrolled way.

CELL
A basic functional structure of an organism.

CONTAGIOUS
Spreading easily from one organism to another.

INFECTIOUS

Causing disease and easily passed from one person to another.

RATION

To limit something that can be given or sold to individuals.

RETRACT

To withdraw from publication.

SEIZURE

A surge of electrical energy in the brain that causes a variety of symptoms, from jerky movements to sudden stillness.

SIDE EFFECT

An unintended result of a medical treatment.

ADDITIONAL
RESOURCES

SELECTED BIBLIOGRAPHY

"History of Anti-Vaccination Movements." *History of Vaccines.*
The College of Physicians of Philadelphia, 18 December 2014.
Web. 2 Mar. 2015.

"State of the World's Vaccines and Immunizations." *UNICEF.*
UNICEF, 2009. Web. 3 Mar. 2015.

FURTHER READINGS

Allman, Toney. *Vaccine Research.* San Diego, CA:
ReferencePoint, 2010. Print.

Hand, Carol. *Vaccines.* Minneapolis, MN: Abdo, 2014. Print.

Hillstrom, Laurie. *Vaccines.* San Diego, CA: Lucent, 2012. Print.

WEBSITES

To learn more about Special Reports, visit **booklinks.abdopublishing.com**. These links are routinely monitored and updated to provide the most current information available.

FOR MORE INFORMATION

For more information on this subject, contact or visit the following organizations:

Centers for Disease Control and Prevention (CDC)
1600 Clifton Road
Atlanta, GA 30329
800-CDC-INFO
http://www.cdc.gov
The CDC works to protect Americans from health and safety threats, such as infectious diseases.

World Health Organization
525 Twenty-Third Street NW
Washington, DC 20037
202-974-3000
http://www.paho.org/hq
The WHO plays an active role in coordinating health matters for the United Nations. It works to set health-care standards, create health-care policy, and support health-care workers.

SOURCE
NOTES

CHAPTER 1. THE OUTBREAK

1. "Measles Vaccination." *CDC*. CDC, 3 Nov. 2014. Web. 3 Mar. 2015.

2. Lenny Bernstein. "Authorities Still Trying to Determine How Measles Outbreak Began at Disney Theme Park." *Washington Post*. Washington Post, 17 Feb. 2015. Web. 3 Mar. 2015.

3. "Measles Cases and Outbreaks." *CDC*. CDC, 29 May 2015. Web. 5 June 2015.

4. "Transmission of Measles." *CDC*. CDC, 31 March 2015. Web. 5 June 2015.

5. Lenny Bernstein. "Authorities Still Trying to Determine How Measles Outbreak Began at Disney Theme Park." *Washington Post*. Washington Post, 17 Feb. 2015. Web. 3 Mar. 2015.

6. "Measles Prevention." *CDC*. CDC, 29 Dec. 1989. Web. 2 Mar. 2015.

7. Ibid.

8. "Measles Vaccination: Who Needs It?" *CDC*. CDC, 4 Feb. 2015. Web. 3 Mar. 2015.

9. "Data and Statistics." *CDC*. CDC, 26 Feb. 2015. Web. 3 Mar. 2015.

10. "Vaccination Coverage among Children in Kindergarten." *CDC*. CDC, 17 Oct. 2014. Web. 5 June 2015.

11. Maggie Fox. "Disney Measles Outbreak Could Get Worse, Experts Warn." *NBC News*. NBC, 4 Feb. 2015. Web. 3 Mar. 2015.

12. "Mobile Vaccination Clinic Reaches Rural Areas." *Center for Infectious Disease Research and Policy*. University of Minnesota, n.d. Web. 5 June 2015.

13. Jen Kirby. "What Anti-Vaccinators Are Saying About the Disneyland Measles Outbreak." *New York Magazine*. New York Magazine, 3 Feb. 2015. Web. 3 Mar. 2015.

CHAPTER 2. A HISTORY OF CONTROVERSY

1. Kevin Malone and Alan Hinman. "Vaccination Mandates: The Public Health Imperative and Individual Rights." *CDC*. CDC, n.d. Web. 25 Mar. 2015.

2. "History of Anti-Vaccination Movements." *History of Anti-Vaccination Movements.* The College of Physicians of Philadelphia, 18 Dec. 2014. Web. 2 Mar. 2015.

3. "Your Baby's Vaccinations." *March of Dimes.* March of Dimes, 2015. Web. 24 Mar. 2015.

4. Paige Lavender. "Roald Dahl Wrote This Painful Plea For Vaccinations After His Own Daughter Died of Measles." *Huffington Post.* Huffington Post, 2 Feb. 2015. Web. 5 June 2015.

CHAPTER 3. VACCINE ISSUES AND HERD IMMUNITY

1. Michael Fitzpatrick. "The Cutter Incident: How America's First Polio Vaccine Led to a Growing Vaccine Crisis." *Journal of the Royal Society of Medicine* 99.3 (2006): 156. Web. 5 June 2015.

2. Jo Craven McGinty. "How Anti-Vaccination Trends Vex Herd Immunity." *Wall Street Journal.* Wall Street Journal, 6 Feb. 2015. Web. 26 Mar. 2015.

3. G. Chowell, M. A. Miller, and C. Viboud. "Seasonal Influenza in the United States, France, and Australia: Transmission and Prospects for Control." *Epidemiology and Infection* 136.6 (2008): 852–864. Web. 5 June 2015.

4. Laura Lorenzetti. "Why You Should Care about the Measles Outbreak." *Fortune.* Fortune, 30 Jan. 2015. Web. 25 Mar. 2015.

CHAPTER 4. VACCINES AND POPULAR CULTURE

1. Declan McCullagh. "Healthcare Workers Protest Mandatory H1N1 Vaccination." *CBS News.* CBS, 29 Sept. 2009. Web. 25 Mar. 2015.

2. "About the VAERS Program." *VAERS.* US Department of Health and Human Services, n.d. Web. 5 June 2015.

3. Eliza Barclay. "Vaccine Mistrust Spreading to the Developing World." *NPR.* NPR, 25 July 2011. Web. 4 Mar. 2015.

4. Chiderah Monde. "Alicia Silverstone's 'Kind Mama' Parenting Book Sparks Controversy for Advice against Diapers, Tampons." *New York Daily News.* New York Daily News, 27 Apr. 2014. Web. 25 Mar. 2015.

5. Jenny McCarthy. "Who's Afraid of the Big Bad Truth?" *Huffington Post.* Huffington Post, 9 May 2010. Web. 3 Mar. 2015.

6. Jenny McCarthy. "The Gray Area on Vaccines." *Chicago Sun-Times.* Chicago Sun-Times, 14 May 2014. Web. 25 Mar. 2015.

7. Noah Gray. "Why Does Donald Trump Think Vaccines Cause Autism?" *Huffington Post.* Huffington Post, 13 Apr. 2012. Web. 28 Mar. 2015.

CHAPTER 5. MAKING VACCINES

1. "Immunization Coverage." *WHO.* WHO, Nov. 2014. Web. 25 Mar. 2015.

2. "CDC Whistle Blower." *Snopes.* Snopes, 3 Feb. 2015. Web. 5 June 2015.

3. Bourree Lam. "Vaccines Are Profitable, So What?" *Atlantic.* Atlantic, 10 Feb. 2015. Web. 5 June 2015.

SOURCE NOTES
CONTINUED

4. "Rotavirus Vaccine and Intussusception." *CDC*. CDC, 8 Apr. 2014. Web. 25 Mar. 2015.

5. Molly Billings. "The Influenza Pandemic of 1918." *Stanford*. Stanford, Feb. 2005. Web. 5 June 2015.

6. "The 2009 H1N1 Pandemic." *CDC*. CDC, 3 Aug. 2010. Web. 25 Mar. 2015.

CHAPTER 6. NEW VACCINES, NEW WORRIES

1. Liz Szabo. "To Ward Off Flu: Shot or Nasal Spray? Depends on Age." *USA Today*. USA Today, 3 Nov. 2012. Web. 5 June 2015.

2. Elizabeth Armstrong Moore. "Microneedle Patches Could Make a Flu Shot as Simple as a Bandaid." *Gigaom*. Gigaom, 24 Nov. 2014. Web. 25 Mar. 2015.

3. Kelley King Heyworth. "Vaccines: The Reality Behind the Debate." *Parents*. Parents, n.d. Web. 3 Mar. 2015.

4. Barbara A. Slade et al. "Postlicensure Safety Surveillance for Quadrivalent Human Papillomavirus Recombinant Vaccine." *Journal of the American Medical Association* 302.7 (2009). Web. 5 June 2015.

5. Ibid.

6. Robyn Carlyle. "How Accurate Are the Recent Claims of Dangers of the HPV-Vaccination Gardasil?" *Huffington Post*. Huffington Post, 25 Oct. 2013. Web. 25 Mar. 2015.

7. Ellen Uchimiya. "Ted Cruz Calls Vaccine Issue 'Largely Silliness Stirred Up by the Media.'" *CBS News*. CBS News, 2 Feb. 2015. Web. 25 Mar. 2015.

8. Ibid.

9. Ibid.

10. "Dr. Bob Sears in the New York Times." *Ask Dr. Sears*. Ask Dr. Sears, 14 Nov. 2007. Web. 5 June 2015.

11. Angie Drobnic and Louis Jacobson. "Michelle Bachman Says HPV Vaccine Can Cause Mental Retardation." *PolitiFact*. Tampa Bay Times, 16 Sept. 2011. Web. 25 Mar. 2015.

CHAPTER 7. THE GLOBAL IMPACT OF VACCINES

1. "State of the World's Vaccines and Immunizations." *UNICEF*. UNICEF, 2009. Web. 3 Mar. 2015.

2. Geoff Deane. "From TED to China." *Intellectual Adventures Lab*. Intellectual Adventures Lab, 9 July 2013. Web. 25 Mar. 2015.

3. "Rubella Case: MOH Tracing Contacts." *Asia One*. Straits Times, 22 Mar. 2015. Web. 25 Mar. 2015.

4. "Fact Sheet: US Response to the Ebola Epidemic in Africa." *White House*. White House, 16 Sept. 2014. Web. 25 Mar. 2015.

5. James Maynard. "Vaccine Costs in Developing Countries Too High, Many Blame GSK, Pfizer." *Tech Times*. Tech Times, 22 Jan. 2015. Web. Mar. 2015.

6. Sarah Boseley. "Pharmaceutical Companies Told to Slash Price of Pneumococcal Disease." *Guardian*. Guardian, 20 Jan. 2015. Web. 25 Mar. 2015.

7. "State of the World's Vaccines and Immunizations." *UNICEF*. UNICEF, 2009. Web. 3 Mar. 2015.

8. "Vaccine Delivery: Strategic Overview." *Gates Foundation*. Gates Foundation, n.d. Web. 25 Mar. 2015.

9. "Who We Are: History." *Gates Foundation*. Gates Foundation, n.d. Web. 25 Mar. 2015.

10. "State of the World's Vaccines and Immunizations." *UNICEF*. UNICEF, 2009. Web. 3 Mar. 2015.

11. Erik Sherman. "Here's the Money behind the Anti-Vaccine Movement." *Daily Finance*. Daily Finance, 6 Feb. 2015. Web. 25 Mar. 2015.

CHAPTER 8. THE FUTURE OF THE VACCINE DEBATE

1. "Vaccine Laws." *NVIC*. NVIC, 2015. Web. 25 Mar. 2015.

2. Lydia O'Connor. "Do Not Bring Your Kids to Measles Parties, Doctors Warn." *Huffington Post*. Huffington Post, 11 Feb. 2015. Web. 25 Mar. 2015.

3. "Finally, the Anti-Vaccine Movement Is Losing Steam." *LA Times*. LA Times, 23 Dec. 2015. Web. 25 Mar. 2015.

4. Ibid.

5. Todd Ackerman. "Amid Measles Outbreaks, Non-Vaccination Movement Grows." *Houston Chronicle*. Houston Chronicle, 4 Feb. 2015. Web. 25 Mar. 2015.

6. Merrill Goozner. *The $800 Million Pill: The Truth Behind the Cost of New Drugs*. Berkeley, CA: U of California P, 2004. Print. 230.

7. Hannah Semigran. "Altruism and Profit: The Changing Role of Pharmaceutical Companies in Global Health." *Harvard College Global Health Review*. Harvard College, 1 Feb. 2012. Web. 5 June 2015.

8. Barry Leibowitz. "Supreme Court Vaccine Ruling: Parents Can't Sue Drug Makers for Kids' Health Problems." *CBS News*. CBS News, 23 Feb. 2011. Web. 15 Mar. 2015.

9. John LaMattina. "Pharma's Reputation Continues to Suffer: What Can Be Done to Fix It?" *Forbes*. Forbes, 18 Jan. 2013. Web. 25 Mar. 2015.

INDEX

ABOUT THE
AUTHOR

Rebecca Rissman is an award-winning children's author and editor. Her writing has been praised by *School Library Journal*, *Booklist*, *Creative Child Magazine*, and *Learning Magazine*. She has written more than 200 books about history, culture, science, and art. She lives in Portland, Oregon, with her husband and daughter.